Rosa's Journey

by Pamela Rushby

EDUCATORS PUBLISHING SERVICE
Cambridge and Toronto

Series Authors: Kay Kovalevs and Alison Dewsbury
Commissioning Editors: Rachel Elliott, Tom Beran, Lynn Robbins, and Laura Woollett
Text by Pamela Rushby
Illustrated by Brian Harrison
Edited by Marcy Gilbert and Sandra Balonyi
Text designed by Andrea Jaretzki and Regine Abos
Cover designed by Kathryn Greenough

Making Connections® developed by Educators Publishing Service, a division of School Specialty Publishing, and Pearson Education Australia, a division of Pearson Australia Group Pty Ltd.

ISBN 978 0 8388 3348 3

1 2 3 4 5 PEA 12 11 10 09 08

Printed in China.

Contents

Chapter 1
The Letter

It was a warm day, and we were outside working on the farm. We all looked up when we heard our neighbor calling. He was waving something in the air. "A letter for you!" he called. "A letter all the way from America!"

Nonno, my grandpa, took the letter from him, and we all crowded around. We knew it was a letter from Uncle Alberto, my uncle who had gone to America. Everyone wanted to hear his news.

Nonno opened the envelope, and a photograph fell out. We gasped. A photograph! Uncle Alberto had sent us letters before, but he had never sent a photograph. I hadn't seen him since he left Italy when I was a little girl. I was starting to forget what he looked like.

The picture reminded me. In the photograph, a young man in a suit was sitting on a chair. He had a straw hat in his hand. He looked serious, but I remembered how much fun Uncle Alberto was. I missed him.

Nonna, my grandma, missed him, too. She seized the photograph and smiled. "Oh!" she cried. "My baby! My Alberto! See how rich he looks!"

Nonna hugged the photograph, and Nonno handed the letter to my younger brother Carlo. "Please read it for us, Carlo," he said.

Carlo was the only one in the family who knew how to read. He was smart, so he had gone to school for a few years. But this year Papa and Mama couldn't afford to pay for school anymore. We only had enough money to buy the food that we couldn't grow ourselves. Sometimes there wasn't even enough money for that.

Carlo took the letter from Nonno. "My dear family," he read. "I have wonderful

news! I have bought a small farm. It
is in a beautiful part of California, not
far from where I have been working at
Signor Brown's farm. It is a very small
farm, but it is mine.

"I want to invite one of my brothers to
join me in America. He could bring his
family and work on my farm. Soon he
would have enough money to buy a farm
of his own. What do you think? It would
make me so happy to have family here in
America! Love, Alberto."

We all looked at each other. I knew
there was no question. Of course one of
the families would go. I held my breath.
It would be so exciting to travel across
the ocean! But would it be my family? Or
would Uncle Antonio's family go?

Late that night, I heard everyone talking. All of the children had already gone to bed, including me. The grown-ups—Nonno and Nonna, my aunt and uncle, and Papa and Mama—sat around the big table in the kitchen. They talked for a long time.

I wanted to hear what they were saying, so I listened hard from my bed. "Our children are so young," said Aunt Gina. "I'd be afraid to take my babies over the sea."

"Maria and Giorgio are little, too," said Mama. Maria and Giorgio were the babies. They were only four and five years old that year. "But Rosa is fourteen now. She would be able to help me."

"And Carlo," said Nonno. "Think of Carlo. Maybe Carlo could go back to school. Maybe all the children could go."

"They say the streets in America are paved with gold," Nonna said. "Alberto is rich. Everyone in America must be rich!"

"If you go now," Uncle Antonio said to Papa, "you could buy a farm soon, too. Then, when our children are older, Gina and I could come."

It was silent for a moment. "Then we will be all alone," Nonna said softly.

It was silent again. "Well, then you will have to come, too," Mama said. Her voice sounded firm. "Italy is our home. Yes, it will be hard to leave. But at least, in America, our children will have food to eat every day."

Chapter 2
So Far Away

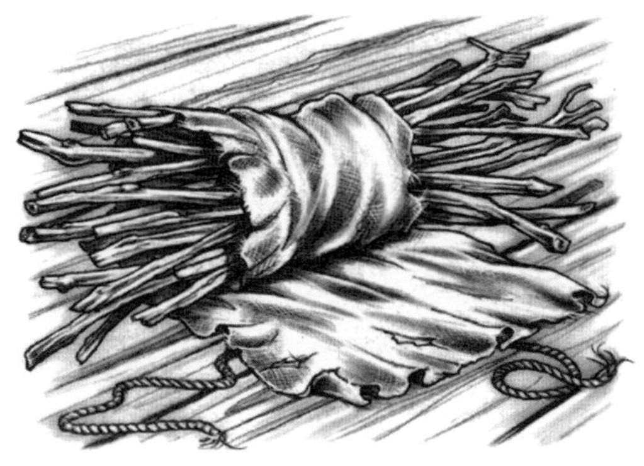

The next few months flew by. Carlo wrote to Uncle Alberto for Papa and said we would come. Then Uncle Alberto wrote again and sent real American dollars! We had never seen American dollars before. Papa would use the money

to pay for our tickets. We needed tickets
for the ship to America and also for the
train from New York to California.

Carlo borrowed a book of maps,
called an atlas, from his old teacher. He
pointed out New York. Then he pointed
to California, all the way on the other
side of the country.

"How far is it from New York to
California?" I asked. "As far as Rome?" I
didn't know of any place in Italy that was
farther away than Rome.

"No," Carlo said. "Much farther." He
showed us how small Italy was, compared
to America. "So big!" we all said.

Then Carlo showed us the huge ocean
between Italy and America. Nonna
started to weep.

"You'll be so far away!" she cried.

I hugged her. "We'll send you letters," I said. "And maybe even a photograph!" I imagined wearing my best dress and sitting very still for the camera. If Uncle Alberto could have his photograph taken, we could, too!

Nonna cried again the day we left. So did Mama and Aunt Gina. Papa, Uncle Antonio, and Nonno hugged each other tightly. They even wiped their eyes.

Then Nonna handed me a package. I opened it up and found a set of beautiful sheets and pillowcases that she had made. "This is for my Rosa," she said. "I wish there was time for me to make more. I made these for your dowry. You'll be thinking about getting married in just a few years. And I won't be there for your wedding!" Her eyes got teary again.

"You'll be there," said Papa. "I'll earn the money for your tickets quickly." He turned to Nonno. "I promise, you'll both dance at Rosa's wedding!"

But Nonna wasn't finished. She also gave us a barrel of pickled vegetables and a sack of dried pasta that she had made. "Here," she said darkly. "You'll need this. You don't know what kind of strange food you'll find in America!"

Nonno handed Papa a bundle. It looked like a bunch of dry sticks that were wrapped in rough, brown fabric. "Cuttings from our grape vines," he explained. "Give them to Alberto, and grow them on his farm. That way, you'll always have a piece of Italy with you."

Chapter 3
A Long Journey

The ship to America was very crowded. We slept close together, deep inside the ship. Many people were seasick. It was hot and stuffy down there, and we went up on deck every time we were allowed.

Papa also had to care for the cuttings we brought from Nonno. He wouldn't let us touch them, but he made sure they stayed damp.

We were on the ship for many weeks. When we finally reached America, we stopped at a place called Ellis Island. At Ellis Island, the American officials would decide whether we could stay in America or if we would be sent back to Italy. It was good that we were all still healthy. It was also good that we had a little money.

Mama held Maria's and Giorgio's hands during the inspection. Carlo and I went together, and Papa went with the bundle of grape cuttings. The officials waved us on.

We had passed the inspection. We could stay! We were so relieved. Mama

hugged Giorgio and Maria tightly. Carlo and I grinned at each other.

Next, we took a ferry to New York. We knew that we should go to the train station and buy our tickets for California. But we didn't know where the train station was. Papa put all our luggage together. He told Mama, Giorgio, and Maria to sit on it.

"Rosa, help Mama with the little ones. You wait here, and Carlo and I will be back soon. We'll find out about the train," he said. "Someone must speak Italian."

Just then a man walked over to us. He spoke Italian! He told us he was from an organization that helped people who came to America from other countries. He helped immigrants like us.

"You want to go to California?" he asked. "So you need railway tickets then. Why don't you stay here with your luggage, and I'll go and buy your tickets for you?"

"*Grazie*, thank you!" said Papa. "What a wonderful country! Everyone wants to help." He gave the man the money for our tickets, and we sat down to wait.

An hour passed, and the man had not returned. We knew something was wrong. Three hours later, we were still sitting there. We had been tricked! That man had taken our money, and he wasn't coming back. Papa and Mama looked desperately at each other. What could we do?

"*Scusa*, excuse me," a voice said. We looked up at a man with a nice face. "I'm from an organization that helps new immigrants," he said. "Do you need some help?"

Papa exploded. "Get away from my family!" he yelled. "This is a terrible country! Americans are all cheats and liars! Go away, go away!"

The man stepped back. But then he managed to calm Papa down. When Papa stopped yelling, we learned that this man really *was* from an organization that helped Italian immigrants. His name was Signor Russo. He said he could help us find a place to stay. We didn't know what else to do, so we went with him.

Chapter 4
A New Life

We went with Signor Russo to an office in a big building. There were a lot of people there. Many were new immigrants like us. Others were people who worked for the organization. Signor Russo explained what had happened to us.

"I'll tell the police about that man," someone else said. "But your money is probably gone. Could your brother send more money?"

Papa shook his head. I knew he wouldn't ask Uncle Alberto for more money. "I'll earn the money for our tickets to California," he said. "Or maybe I'll just earn enough money to go back to Italy. America is a terrible country!"

Mama looked at him. "Not all Americans are terrible," she said quietly. "These people are trying to help us. We won't be tricked again."

"We can help you find a room and a job," Signor Russo said.

They found us a room in an apartment building down a dark, narrow alley. It smelled in the alley and on the stairs. Our

room was on the third floor. The plaster was peeling off the walls, and we had to go to the ground floor to get water.

The room was cheap, though. And I heard people speaking Italian. At least we would be near people we could understand. We moved in.

The next day, I even made a friend. We were scrubbing our room when we heard a knock on the door. I opened it and saw a girl about my own age. She was holding a plate of cookies.

"I'm Donatella," she said in Italian. "I live downstairs. Mama asked me to bring you some *biscotti*."

Mama smiled at her. "Thank your mama," she said. "I'll come and visit her

when this room is clean. Have you lived
in America long?"

"We've been here for four years,"
said Donatella. She smiled at me. "Can I
show you the neighborhood?"

Mama nodded at me, and Donatella
showed Carlo and me around our new
neighborhood. It was full of Italians.

"Americans call this area Little Italy,"
Donatella said. "But there are American
things here, too. There's a school and
a library. I go to English classes at the
library in the evenings."

"A school!" said Carlo. "I want to go
to school!"

"I can show you where it is and
help you sign up," said Donatella. She
turned to me and asked, "Will you go to
school, too?"

I stared at her. "No, I don't think so,"
I said. "I stay home and help Mama. I'd
like to learn English, though."

"Then you'd better come to the classes
at the library with me," Donatella said.
"We can go tonight."

Chapter 5
A Little Piece of Heaven

I was worried about Papa. The people
from the organization did find him a
job. He worked for the city. But he never
talked to us anymore, and he never
played with the little ones. He just came
home, ate quickly, and went to sleep.

Mama asked Carlo to write to Uncle
Alberto and explain what had happened
to the money. Uncle Alberto was sad
when he wrote back. He didn't have any
more money to send us. We would have
to stay and work in New York.

When Carlo asked Papa about
Nonno's grape cuttings, Papa scowled.
"I don't care about those cuttings! I
just want to earn enough money to buy
tickets out of here!" He didn't say if he
meant tickets to California or to Italy.

I tried to keep the cuttings wet, like
Papa had on the ship. But I wasn't sure
what else to do for them. Maybe they
needed sunlight, like plants in the ground.

Donatella said, "Why don't we take
them to the park? We could put them in
the sun."

We had to walk a long way to the park. I held the bundle of cuttings carefully. Finally, we crossed a busy road, and I looked up. I could hardly believe my eyes. Right in the middle of this huge city, there was a little piece of heaven. Everywhere I looked, there were trees and flowers, lakes and rocks.

Grown-ups were walking along the paths, and children were playing on the grass. Some people wore expensive clothes, but lots of people looked like Donatella and me.

Donatella sat down on the grass. I opened the bundle of cuttings and put them in the sun. Then I sat down and tilted my face toward the sun, too.

"Now," said Donatella, "let's practice your English. Tell me the days of the week."

I groaned, but I started anyway. "*Lunedì*—Monday, *martedì*—Tuesday, *mercoledì*—Wednesday ..."

When I finished, Donatella said, "Good. You're learning so fast! You should go to school like Carlo."

"Me?" I said. "Not me! I just want to learn enough English to get a job and help Papa with our tickets."

As I finished talking, I saw a tall, strong-looking boy next to me. He was looking at the grape cuttings that I had put in the sun. I got up to protect them, but he got to them first.

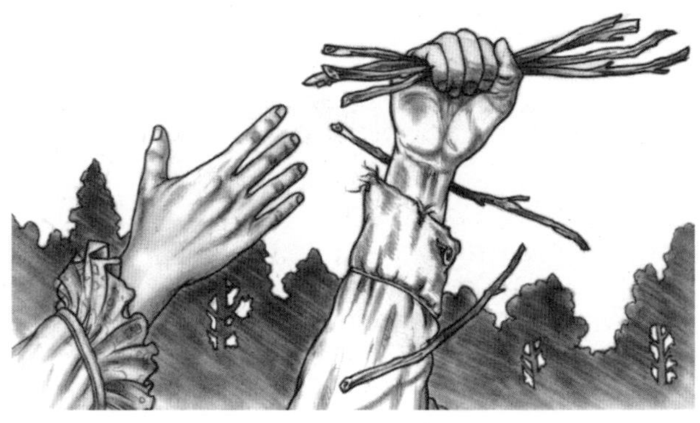

Chapter 6
Rescued!

The boy grabbed one of the cuttings and laughed meanly. "What's this?" he grinned. "Is this your toy? You're playing with sticks and dirt?"

I didn't understand him, but he wasn't going to take our grape cuttings.

"Give that back!" I shouted in Italian.

I heard Donatella echo me in English. "Give that back!"

The boy laughed again and picked up another cutting. He tossed the cuttings from hand to hand. Then he threw two of the larger cuttings over our heads. We spun around. Two other boys were behind us, and they were each holding a cutting.

"Hey, John!" one boy called to the first boy. "It's a baseball bat. You pitch!" He wrapped his hands around one end of the cutting and held it up near his shoulder. Then he swung the cutting around, straightening his arms as he moved.

The third boy laughed and imitated him. "Yeah!" he shouted.

"Give it back!" I shouted in Italian. "It's mine!"

The boys threw the cuttings again, laughing. This time the cuttings landed on the ground. I ran around, trying to gather them up. The one named John raised his boot as if he was going to stamp on one.

"No!" I shouted.

There was a loud smack, and John shouted, too. "Ow!" he howled. A walking stick had rapped him on the ankle.

"What is going on here?"

It was a very proper voice that had spoken. I looked up. A well-dressed man and a beautiful lady were standing near us. The lady looked calm and even smiled at me, but the man was frowning at the boys. He looked mean.

John was rubbing his ankle. The other two boys backed away from us slowly.

"Big boys like you, teasing girls!" the man scolded. "You should be ashamed!" He shook his walking stick, and the boys ran away.

The man picked up some of the cuttings. He had stopped frowning, so he looked nicer. I was still nervous about him, though. Then he asked me something, but I didn't understand.

"He wants to know if they're grape cuttings," Donatella explained.

"Yes," I said in English. Then I switched back to Italian. "They're from our farm in Italy."

Donatella helped me tell the couple the whole story. The man was very interested, especially in the cuttings.

"He says he likes to grow plants," Donatella told me. "He says he has a greenhouse—a special room for growing plants—at his house."

"Can he tell if the cuttings will grow?" I asked hopefully. We had been waiting so long to plant them, and then those boys had thrown them around. I hoped they weren't dead.

The man wasn't sure. But he offered to take them home and plant them in his greenhouse. I wasn't sure about that! I couldn't give the cuttings away. What if it was another trick?

Chapter 7
Will They Grow?

The lady could see that I wasn't
sure what to do. She said something
to Donatella, and Donatella translated
for me. "She says their name is Martin.
They live on Fifth Avenue. She says
we can come to their house and see

the greenhouse. We should bring your mother or father."

Papa was working, of course. When we told Mama, she wasn't sure what to do. But she could see how much I wanted to go to the Martins' house, so she agreed to come. When we finally got to the Martins' house, we didn't know what to do. It was so big. It was like a palace!

The maid who opened the door didn't know what to do either. She did not want to let us in. But I showed her the cuttings, and she went to find Mr. and Mrs. Martin. They took us inside the house and brought us to the greenhouse in the backyard.

The greenhouse was wonderful! It was a separate building from the house, and the walls and roof were made of glass. The sun shone through the glass and made the greenhouse warm. It smelled earthy and wet, too. I could tell the cuttings would be safe there, so I gave them to Mr. Martin to plant.

Mrs. Martin said something to Donatella, and Donatella turned to Mama. "Signora Martin says she needs someone to help with housework," she said. "If you can do the work, she would pay you. What do you think?"

"*Sì*," said Mama. "That would be good."

It was all arranged quickly. Mama went to the Martins' house every day. She helped the housekeeper with the cleaning and did some sewing as well. I took care of Maria and Giorgio. When Mama came home in the evenings, I took English lessons at the library. If we weren't too tired, Carlo would tell us what he had

learned at school that day. Mama and I
practiced English with him.

Papa wasn't very happy. "My wife,
going out to work!" he said with a frown.
"It's not right!"

But Donatella's parents told him it was
all right. "This way, you'll be able to earn
money for your tickets faster," they said.
"Besides, in America, many women do
have jobs."

"Huh! America!" Papa snorted. But he
didn't sound as unhappy about America
as he had before.

Sometimes I went to the Martins'
house myself. I liked to check on the
cuttings. Mr. Martin had put them into
pots. He also gave them special food,
called fertilizer, to help the plants grow
fast and strong.

And then, one day, I could see they were alive! There were small greenish bumps where the new leaves would be. Until that day, the cuttings had just looked like dried-up, old sticks. I was so excited. I felt like a piece of Italy was growing right here in America.

"Thank you! Thank you!" I said to Mr. Martin—in English.

At the end of each week, Papa and Mama got paid. We paid for our room and bought food. Sometimes, Maria or Giorgio needed new clothes. But we saved as much money as we could. Mama put our extra money in a jar. Slowly the number of coins grew.

Chapter 8
The End of the Journey

One day I realized that we had been in New York for almost a year. And at the end of that week, Mama said we had enough money to buy our tickets.

"Which tickets?" Carlo asked. I held my breath. Where would we go?

Papa looked at us. Then he smiled at Mama. He turned to Carlo and said, "You'd better write to Uncle Alberto. We have to let him know we're coming."

Carlo and I cheered. We were staying in America!

The day we left New York, everyone came to the train station. Mr. Martin brought the pots with our cuttings. Papa couldn't believe his eyes.

"I thought they were all dead! *Grazie*, thank you!" he said. He spoke in Italian, but Mr. Martin knew what he meant. He shook Papa's hand.

"When they are growing in California, would you send me some cuttings for my greenhouse?" he asked.

I translated for Papa, and he nodded.
"You will have the first!" Papa promised.

The train whistled. Mr. Martin, Mrs. Martin, Donatella, and Donatella's family all waved as the train started moving. "Write to me!" Donatella called.

"We will!" I shouted.

Soon they disappeared. I was too excited to be sad. We were actually on our way to California.

Papa was also amazed, but for a different reason. He was still staring at the cuttings, looking at them as if they were gold.

"You see?" I said. "There are wonderful people right here in America!"

Papa smiled at me. "But none as wonderful as you, my Rosa," he replied.